# Jokes for Kids

## 250+ Feline Focused Clean One Liners, Riddles, Knock Knock and Would You Rather Jokes For Kids (Funny Gift for Children)

## By
## Seamus Mullarkey

# SPECIAL BONUS!

## Want This Bonus Book for free?

Get **FREE**, unlimited access to it and all of my new books by joining our Fan club!

*SCAN W/ YOUR CAMERA TO JOIN!*

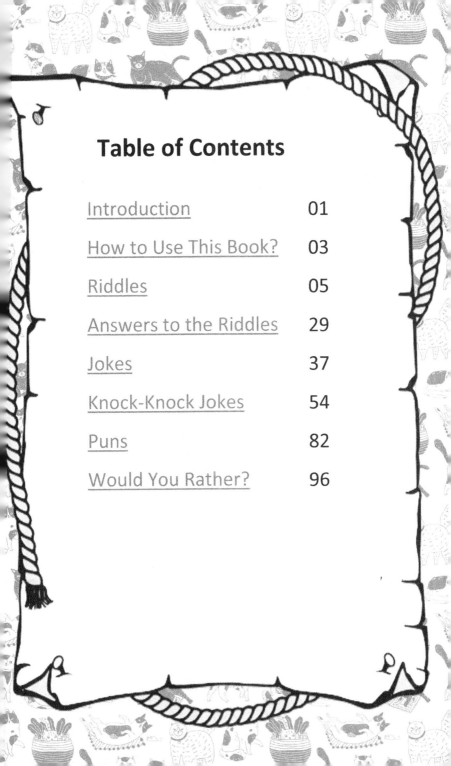

# Table of Contents

# Introduction

Prepare to be entertained! This is going to be a fun and wacky adventure that celebrates the humorous side of our much loved cats.

We've gathered **250** Riddles, Jokes, Knock-Knock's, Puns, and Would You Rathers? about cats that will not only have you and your kids laughing out loud, but will make the time spent with them truly interactive and a great bonding experience. What's more, your kids will keep themselves fully entertained on road trips, vacations, winter holidays and many, many, more occasions.

The different categories will provide a variety of experiences both you and your kids will cherish. We guarantee they won't have a dull moment when reading this book. We know that kids need something extra-fun to occupy themselves and that is why we have made a book with a playful tempo. that switches from one category to another. so that they'll be "glued" to these pages!

HAVE YOU HUGGED YOUR CAT TODAY?

# How To Use This Book

We have made this book easy for kids to understand and the rules are really simple to follow:

As we mentioned. this is a collection of **250** fantastic cat jokes for kids. You can read the book with them. or they can play among themselves.

☒ **For the Riddles section** they need to guess the right answer—if they can!

☒ **For the Jokes section.** they can simply enjoy the hilarious answers.

☒ **The Knock-Knock section** is most fun when read aloud. either you with your child. or one child to another.

☒ **The Puns section** is a simply fun section to read and chuckle at, although it does include some tricky word play to stretch their brains a bit.

☒ **For the Would You Rather questions,** they have to choose one of two options. Some of them might be difficult to decide on, but they'll be laughing away at some of the silly choices.

# Enjoy!

# Riddles

—Answers are on the Answers **To The Riddles** pages.

1. What do you call a cat who has two ears?

2. What do you get when you cross a ball and a cat?

3. How far into the forest can the cat run?

**4.** How do you spell mouse-trap with **ONLY** three letters?

**5.** What would **3/7th** of a chicken, **2/3rd** of a cat, and half of a goat make?

**6.** What does a cat have that no other animal has?

7. A farmer, a horse, and a kitten decide to cross a bridge. The farmer rode across the bridge on his horse, yet walked. How's this possible?

8. A cat had three kittens: January, March and May. What was the mother's name?

**9.** Why aren't cats the best dancers?

**10.** What kind of cats can jump higher than a building?

**11.** A cat called Fluffy is sitting on one side of the lake and her owner, a little girl named Maria is standing on the other side of the lake. Fluffy calls for Maria, and when Maria reaches her, the little girl is dry. How's this possible?

**12.** Two children and four cats were crowded under a big umbrella, why did the cats not get wet?

**13.** How many cats can you place inside an empty basket?

**14.** In a square living room there is a cat in every corner. In front of every cat there are three cats. How many cats are there in total?

**15.** A monkey and a cat were having an argument about who was the smartest. The cat told the monkey it could sit somewhere the monkey could not. The monkey accepted the bet and lost. Where could the cat sit but the monkey could not?

**16.** You have two cats. How can you give one away, yet keep both?

**17.** What would happen if you combined a happy cat and a dangerous fish?

**18.** Why do cats make the best soldiers?

**19.** Which side of the cat has the most fur?

**20.** If five cats catch five mice in five minutes, how long will it take one cat to catch a mouse?

**21.** Three black kittens are running in the same direction. The first black kitten has two black kittens behind her, the second black kitten has one black kitten behind her and one black kitten in front of her, but the third black kitten has one black kitten in front of her and one black kitten behind her too.

What is going on?

**22.** A cat can jump five feet high, but can't jump through a window that is three feet high.
**Why?**

**23.** While the cat was outside, it started to rain a lot. The cat couldn't find any shelter and got completely soaked by the rain, yet not a single hair was wet. How could this be?

**24.** Molly adores cats and keeps some as pets. All but two of them are totally orange. All but two of them are totally black. All but two of them are totally brown. How many cats does Molly have?

**25.** Two cats are sitting in a basket, a really big cat and a really small cat. The really small cat is the son of the really big cat, but the really big cat is not the father of the really small cat.
How can this be?

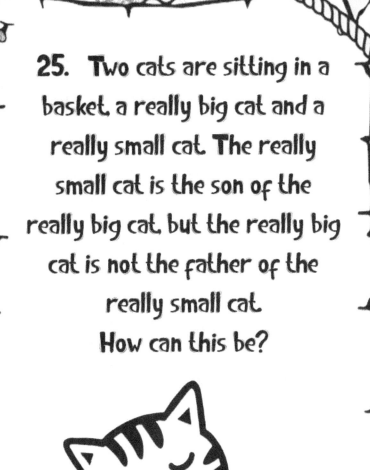

**26.** A beaver is swimming in a pond. A cat is lying on the beaver's back. If the beaver dives under the water, what happens to the cat?

**27.** A kitty can only count to three. 1.2.3 But somehow she knows up to **12** numbers. How is that possible?

**28.** What kind of cat is also a tree?

**29.** When I was going to the store, I met a father with three daughters. Each daughter had two baskets, and in each basket was a mother cat. Each mother cat had three kittens.

How many people were going to the store?

**30.** What kind of a cat goes round the house and through the house but never touches the house?

**31.** Cats have two of them. which are on opposite sides yet never see each other. What am I talking about?

**32.** How can you have one cat, but see two cats?

**33.** What two things can a cat never eat for breakfast?

**34.** A mama cat has five female kittens. Each of these kittens has a brother. How many kittens does the mama cat have?

**35.** A little orange tabby has a basket with three apples. She takes away two. How many apples does the little orange tabby have?

FRESH APPLES!

**36.** A cat in Los Angeles is called Lili. A cat in New York is called Lala. What do you call a cat at the South Pole?

**37.** What question can't a cat answer?

**38.** What do you have to be careful of when it rains cats and dogs?

**39.** What kind of cat is also a ghost?

**40.** What cats purr the best?

**41.** A cat is carrying something. It begins with an " e" and only contains one letter. What is it?

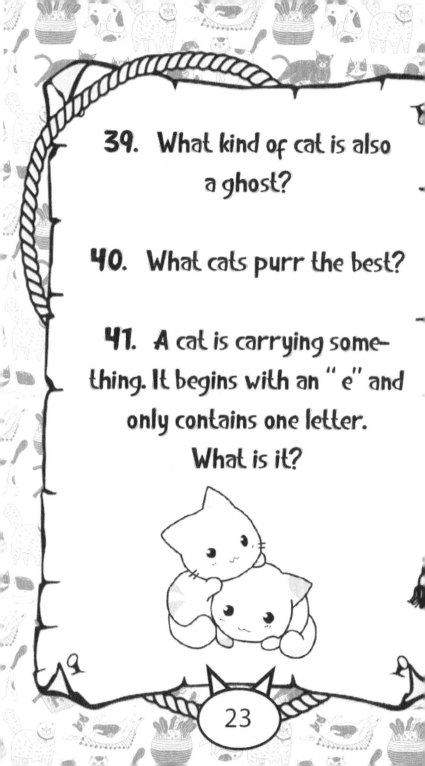

**42.** A cat grabbed something from the kitchen, but then she started crying.
What did she take?

**43.** If you throw your cat in the blue sea, what would it become?

**44.** What's big as a cat, but weighs nothing at all?

**45.** What can a cat hold in her right hand but never in her left hand?

**46.** A cowboy cat arrives in town on Friday. He stays at a local hotel for three nights. He leaves on Friday. What is going on?

**47.** A cat is sitting in her cabin in Minnesota. In less than three hours, she's in her cabin in Texas. How can this be?

**48.** What is always on the cat's dinner table but she cannot eat it?

**49.** A young boy has to transport three animals from one side of a river to the other. These animals are a mouse, a cat, and a dog. However, if he takes the dog with him, while he's gone, the cat will gobble up the mouse. If he takes the mouse with him, the dog will eat the cat. How could he possibly get all three animals across the river while keeping them all alive?

**50.** What is black, white, and blue?

## Answers To the Riddles

1. It doesn't matter. Cats don't usually come when you call.
2. A fur ball.
3. The cat can only run halfway into the forest. This is because if she runs any more she will actually be running out of the forest instead of into it.
4. C-A-T!
5. Chicago. That's because 3/7th of chicken is CHI. 2/3rd of a cat is CA. and half of goat is GO!

6. Kittens

7. It turns out the cat was called "yet."

8. "What" was the mother's name.

9. Because they have two left feet!

10. It doesn't matter what kind of cats. Buildings can't jump.

11. The lake is frozen.

12. It wasn't raining.

13. Only one. Once you put one in it the basket isn't empty any more.

14. Four cats.

15. On the monkey's head.

**16.** Give one away and rename the last cat "Both."

**17.** You'd get a purr-anha.

**18.** It's more difficult to kill them as they have nine lives.

**19.** The outside.

**20.** Five minutes.

**21.** The three black kittens are walking in a circle.

**22.** The window is closed.

**23.** It was a hairless cat.

**24.** 3 - 1 orange, 1 black, 1 brown

**25.** The really big cat is the mother of the really small cat.

26. The cat gets wet.

27. She can count to **3** in different languages (English, Japanese, Spanish and French)

28. A cat-a-log.

29. Just one. Me. I was the one going to the store.

30. A flying cat.

31. Eyes.

32. By holding your cat in front of a mirror.

33. Lunch and dinner.

34. She has six kittens. Each female kitten has the same brother.

**35.** Two apples. She took two and left one in the basket.

**36.** Lost.

**37.** Are you asleep yet?

**38.** Stepping in a poodle.

**39.** A scaredy cat.

**40.** Purr-sians.

**41.** An envelope.

**42.** An onion.

**43.** Wet.

**44.** A cat's shadow.

**45.** Her left hand.

**46.** The cowboy cat has a horse called Friday.

**47.** The cat is a pilot and she is sitting in the cabin of her plane.

**48.** The plate.

**49.** The first step is to take the cat across the river, next he must go back and take the mouse across. He doesn't leave the cat and the mouse alone, but brings the cat back with him and exchanges it for the dog. This leaves the dog and the mouse together (the dog won't eat the mouse) while he goes to fetch the cat. That's it! Mission accomplished.

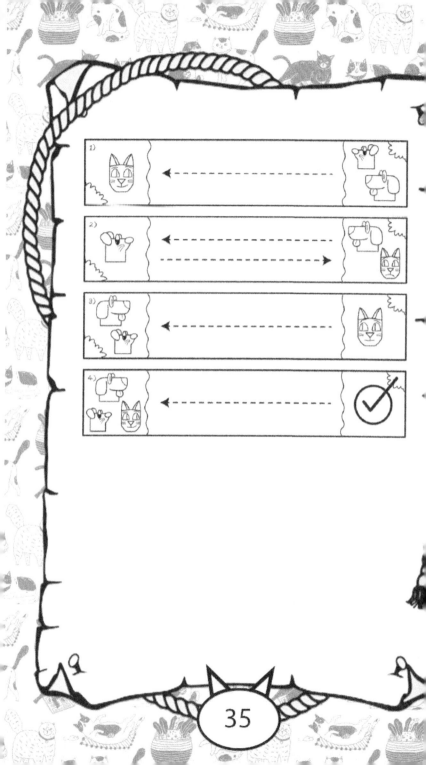

**50.** A black and white cat who's sad.

# Jokes

1. Why are cats good part-
ners to play video
games with?
They have nine lives.

2. What is a cat's
favorite color?
Purrr-ple.

3. What game does a cat
like to play with a mouse?
Catch.

**4.** Where do cats go on a field trip?

To the mews-seum.

**5.** Why do cats go to medical school?

To become first aid kits.

**6.** What state has lots of cats?

Pets-ylvania.

7. Why do cats always get their way?
They are very purr-sua-sive.

8. What is a cat's favorite movie?
The Sound of Mew-sic.

9. Why was the cat so upset?
Because he was in a bad mewd.

**10.** What do baby cats wear instead of using the litter box?
Dia-purrs.

**11.** Why was the cat using the computer for hours on end?
He wanted to keep an eye on the mouse.

**12.** Why can't a group of cats get together to play cards?

There are too many cheetahs.

13. What do you call a pile
of kittens?
A meow-ntain.

14. What would a cat say after
teasing you?
"Just kitten!"

**15.** How does a cat decide what he wants from the store?
He flips through the cat-alog.

**16.** What's it called when all the cat treats are gone?
A cat-astrophe.

**17.** Which day of the week do cats love the most?
Cat-urday.

**18.** Why was the cat afraid of the tree?
Because of its bark.

**19.** What was the cat's least favorite subject in school?
Hisss-tory.

**20.** What do cats have to do in the morning?
Read the mews-paper.

21. How do cats solve
an argument?
Hiss and make up.

22. What happened when
the lion ate the clown?
He felt funny!

23. What kind of cats like
to go bowling?
Alley cats!

**24.** When is it very bad luck to see a black cat?
When you're a mouse!

**25.** What kind of cat works as a gardener?
A lawn-meow-er.

**26.** What does a kitten become after it's three days old?
Four days old!

**27.** Why did the cat put the letter "M" into the freezer? Because it turns "ice" into "mice"!

**28.** If cars run on gas or electricity, what does a cat run on? Its paws!

**29.** What do you call a cat with eight legs that likes to swim? An octo-puss!

**30.** What do you call a cat who rides around in a Honda Civic?
A car-pet.

**31.** Why did the policeman make the cat pay a fine?
Because it littered.

**32.** Why do cats make terrible story tellers?
They only have one "tail."

**34.** What happened after the cat gobbled up a ball of wool?

She had some mittens.

**35.** What do you get when you cross a cat with a parrot?

A carrot.

**36.** How do cats eat spaghetti?

With their mouths—just like everyone else.

**37.** What do cats drive?
A cat-ill-ac.

**38.** What did the cat say when he lost all his money?
"Boo-hoo. I'm so paw."

**39.** What do you call a scary sailor with a cat on his shoulder?
A purr-ate.

**40.** Where can your cat sit that you can't?
Your lap.

**41.** What's the first thing a cat does in the morning?
It wakes up.

**42.** What do you call an old cat?

Grand-paw.

**43.** How do you know your cat used your computer?

Your mouse has teeth marks on it.

**44.** How does a cat count?

Mew, mew-mew,
mew-mew-mew...

**45.** What kind of cat do you want with you in a remote desert?
A survival kit.

**46.** Why do cats on the beach wear red suits and say "Ho, ho, ho"?
Because they've got Sandy Claws!

**47.** How is a cat like a coin?
It has a head on one side and tail on the other side.

**48.** How does a cat
sing scales?
Do-re-me-ow

**49.** What happened when
the cat swallowed
the quarter?
There was money in
the kitty.

**50.** How do you spell cat
backwards?
C-A-T B-A-C-K-W-A-R-D-S

# Knock-Knock Jokes

1. Knock-Knock!
   Who's there?
   Puss.
   Puss who?
   Puss n' Boots!

2. Knock-Knock!
   Who's there?
   Catskills.
   Catskills who?
   Catskills mice.

**3.** Knock-Knock!
Who's there?
Cat.
Cat who?
Cat you understand a word I'm saying? I'm meowing very clearly.

**4.** Knock-Knock!
Who's there?
Hans.
Hans who?
Hans off my cat food!

**5.** Knock-Knock!
Who's there?
Hello.
Hello who?
Hello Kitty!

**6.** Knock-Knock!
Who's there?
Claws.
Claws who?
Claws the door. I am getting cold!

7.  Knock-Knock!
Who's there?
Lion.
Lion who?
Lion around while I'm wait-
ing for you to open the
door is pretty boring!

8.  Knock-Knock!
Who's there?
Puss.
Puss who?
Puss-ibly the most me-
ow-velous cat ever!

**9.** Knock-Knock
Who's there?
Claws.
Claws who?
Santa Claws!

**10.** Knock-Knock
Who's there?
Furry.
Furry who?
It's your Furry Godmoth-
er. Hurry up, you're late
for the ball!

**11.** Knock-Knock!

Who's there?

Claw.

Claw who?

It's Claw Enforcement. You have the right to remain silent. Anything you say or do may be used against you in a court of meow!

**12.** Knock-Knock!

Who's there?

Puss.

Puss who?

Puss me the ketchup. I want to put some on my mouse burger!

**13.** Knock-Knock!
Who's there?
Ben!
Ben who?
Ben down so you can hear me better! I'm just a short little kitty.

**14.** Knock-Knock!
Who's there?
Juan!
Juan who?
Juan-der what the neighbors think of you talking to a cat!

**15.** Knock-knock!
Who's there?
Catsup!
Catsup who?
Catsup on top of the tree and won't come down!

**16.** Knock-Knock!

Who's there?

Purr.

Purr who?

Purr-sonaly, I think when you see how sweet a cat I am you'll adopt me!

**17.** Knock-Knock!

Who's there?

Howie!

Howie who?

Howie like that? It's almost feeding time.

**18.** knock-knock!
Who's there?
Ice cream!
Ice cream who?
Ice cream really loud if you
don't let me in!

**19.** knock-knock!
Who's there?
Thank!
Thank who?
You're welcome! Meow!

**20.** Knock-Knock!
Who's there?
Luke!
Luke who?
Luke out! You almost
stepped on my paw!

**21.** Knock-Knock!
Who's there?
Frank!
Frank who?
Frank you for all the
belly scratches you give
me!

**23.** Knock- knock!
Who's there?
Kitten!
Kitten who?
Quit kitten around and
open the door!

**24.** Knock-knock!
Who's there?
Nobel!
Nobel who?
Nobel...That's why I
knocked and meowed!

**25.** Knock-knock!
Who's there?
Annie.
Annie who?
Annie way you can pet
me?

**26.** Knock-knock!
Who's there?
Hal
Hal who?
Hal will you know if you
don't open the door? It's
me. your kitty!

**26.**    Knock-knock!
Who's there?
Says.
Says who?
Says me. Meow!

**27.**    Knock-knock!
Who's there?
Hawaii.
Hawaii who?
I lost my cat toy, so I'm
pretty annoyed. How are
you?

**28. Knock-knock!**
Who's there?
Orange!
Orange who?
Orange you glad to see me? I'm the cutest cat in town.

Cute_Kitty

#ADORABLE

1,237 LIKES 👍

**29.** Knock-Knock
Who's there?
Woo.
Woo who?
Glad you're excited to see
me. meow!

**30.** Knock-Knock!
Who's there?
Anita.
Anita who?
Let me in. Anita drink my
milk. meow!

**31.** Knock-Knock!
Who's there?
Water.
Water who?
Water you doing opening
the door for stray cats.
don't you have better
things to do?

**32.** Knock-Knock!
Who's there?
Leaf.
Leaf who?
Leaf me alone. Hiss!

**33.** Knock-knock!
Who's there?
Annie.
Annie who?
Annie way you can get a
cat door? I'm sick of
knocking.

**34.** Knock-knock!
Who's there?
Nana.
Nana who?
Nana of your business.
meow!

**35.** Knock-Knock!

Who's there?

Canoe.

Canoe who?

Canoe come out and play with a little kitty?

**36.** Knock-Knock!
Who's there?
Fur.
Fur who?
Fur-got my key. Sorry!

**37.** Knock-Knock
Who's there?
Dozen.
Dozen who?
Dozen anybody want to let
me in? Meow!

**38.** Knock-Knock!
Who's there?
Lettuce.
Lettuce who?
Lettuce in, it's cold out here, it's me and the kittens!

**39.** Knock-Knock!
Who's there?
Amarillo.
Amarillo who?
Amarillo nice cat.

**40.** Knock-knock!
Who's there?
Won.
Won who?
Won-der what took you so long? We cats get impatient, you know!

**41.** Knock- knock!
Who's there?
Police.
Police who?
Police let me in. It's cold outside, meow!

**42.** Knock-Knock
Who's there?
Etch.
Etch who?
Bless you. meow!

**43.** Knock-Knock!
Who's there?
Stopwatch.
Stopwatch who?
Stopwatch you're doing
and let me and my
kittens in!

**44.** Knock-Knock!

Who's there?

Spell.

Spell who?

W.H.O. Meoww!

**45.** Knock-Knock!

Who's there?

Icy.

Icy who?

Icy you hiding that cat

treat from me, meow!

**46.** Knock-Knock!
Who's there?
Mary.
Mary who?
Mary Christmas, meow!

**47.** Knock-knock!
Who's there?
Iva.
Iva who?
Iva sore paw from knocking
and scratching. meow!

**48.** Knock-knock!
Who's there?
Needle.
Needle who?
Needle little furry
company?

**49.** Knock-Knock!
Who's there?
Norma Lee.
Norma Lee who?
Norma Lee I don't knock on random doors, but I'd like you to be my new owner, meow!

**50.** Knock-Knock!
Who's there?
Yukon.
Yukon who?
Yukon go and buy me a new cat bed. The old one really sucks!

# Puns

1. Why are cat toys
never hungry?
They are always stuffed.

2. What would a cat order
in a Mexican restaurant?
A purr-rito.

3. How does a cat invite
fishes to her birthday party?
You are o-fish-ally invited!

**4.** Why are cats
usually stressed?
It is not easy being purr-fect.

**5.** What did the cat say when it
saw Mount Everest?
Look at that meown-tain!

**6.** Why do cats travel
to Egypt?
They love those purrr-amids!

**7.** Why do we like kittens?
It's their cat-titude!

8. What did the confident cat say?
Looking good, feline fine!

9. What do you call a cat who lives underwater?
A little meow-maid.

**10.** What did the vet say to the cat?

I believe you haven't been feline very well.

**11.** Hey kitty, are you sure you want some kibble?

Def-fur-nately!

**12.** What do you call a cat that plays the harmonica?

Har-meow-nious.

**13.** What do you call cat criminals?

Purr-patrators.

**14.** What's a cat's favorite drink?
Cat-puccino!

**15.** Why did the cat slouch?
It had bad paws-ture.

**16.** Why wasn't the cat self-confident?
It had an in-furr-iority complex.

**17.** What do cats dress up as on Halloween?
Vam-purrs!

**18.** Why do cats like funny songs?
Because they're a-mews-sing.

**19.** How do you know your cat likes litter-ature?
It reads "The Great Cats-by."

**20.** What's a cat's most important characteristic?
Its purrsonality.

**21.** Why couldn't the cat use its credit card to buy a **99**c can of cat food?
The store had a **$3.00** me-own-imum purr-chase policy.

**22.** Why was the cat embarrassed?
It forgot its best friend's purr-thday!

**23.** Why don't cats want to improve?
They think they are purr-fect just the way they are!

**24.** Why is it illegal for cats to drive a car?
They could cause a cat-astrophe!

**25.** What do cats paint?
Paw-traits.

**26.** What do cats wear
at night?
Paw-jamas.

**27.** Why was the cat homesick?
It missed its fur-miliar
surroundings.

**28.** What did the cat say to
Santa Claus?
Meow-y Christmas!

**29.** What's a cat's favorite sushi?
Cat-lifornia-drool.

**30.** Why was the cat studying on Sunday night?
It had a test on Meow-nday!

**31.** What do cats say if you get good grades?
Con-cat-ulations!

**32.** Why did the cat go to jail after killing a mouse?
It was guilty of fur-st degree purr-der.

**33.** Why was the cat always grouchy?
It was a sour puss.

**34.** What do cats drink when they don't want to stay awake at night?
De-cat!

**35.** What do cats say on New Year's Eve?
Let's Paw-ty!

**36.** What does a cat say when she really can't do something?
I litter-ally can't!

**37.** Why do cats bug their owners all the time?

Because they're purr-manently hungry!

**38.** Why couldn't the cat play the violin?

It wasn't a mew-sician.

**39.** Why are cats optimistic?

They think paws-itively.

**40.** What do you call a cat marshmallow?

Marsh-meow-llow!

**41.** What do you say to the cat who has it all?

You're very fur-tunate.

**42.** Why is your cat such a snob?

She's an aristo-cat!

**43.** Why do cats make such good comedians?

They're paws-itively hiss-terical.

....SO I SEZ 'HEY! FIND YOUR OWN PIGEON!'

**44.** What do cats say when you get top grades?
How claw-some is that?

**45.** What do polite cats say?
Have a mice day!

**46.** What do cats say when they bump into you?
Purr-don me!

**47.** Why do cats hold grudges?
Because they never fur-get.

**48.** Why did the cat have so many library fines?
It kept its books out fur-ever.

**49.** Does your cat have expensive tastes?
Yes, it wants a Furr-ari!

**50.** Why don't cats fly air-planes?
Because it's im-paws-ible

# Would You Rather?

**1.** Would you rather be able to speak cat language but not be able to talk to humans or to be able to communicate with humans but never have a cat?

**2.** Would you rather be a stray cat and be free to have adventures or a house cat who was always cozy and warm?

**3.** Would you rather have a cat with two tails or one with five legs?

**4.** Would you rather have a crazy cat who bugs you all night or a boring cat that sleeps all day?

**5.** Would you rather have nine lives as a cat does or be able to jump from tree to tree?

**6.** Would you rather be a cat who was hairless or one who had big fluffy fur?

**7.** Would you rather have a cat that acts like a dog or a dog that acts like a cat?

**8.** Would you rather eat your cat's food or a rotten tomato?

**9.** Would you rather have a cat's face or a werewolf's?

**10.** Would you rather be your cat for one day or for your cat to be you for one day?

**11.** Would you rather have a cat with huge dog ears or a cat with a curly tail?

**12.** Would you rather have a tiny kitty you could hold in your hand or a giant cat who was as big as you?

**13.** Would you rather have a really cute cat who was unfriendly or a really friendly cat who was very ugly?

**14.** Would you rather have a cat that cannot stop scratching the furniture or a cat that cannot stop meowing?

**15.** Would you rather have a hamster-size cat or a cat-sized hamster?

**16.** Would you rather have **100** cats or no cats at all?

**17.** Would you rather have a cat who stole your dinner or a cat who stole your phone?

**18.** Would you rather be stuck in a cage with **400** cats or be alone for the rest of your life?

**19.** Would you rather live with two wild cats or have **200** house cats?

**20.** Would you rather read the minds of humans or read the minds of cats?

**21.** Would you rather have a cat from a pet shop or from a pet shelter?

**22.** Would you rather play with your cat or play with your friends?

**23.** Would you rather have your cat yawn all the time or burp all the time?

**24.** Would you rather a cat as big as a horse or a horse as small as a cat?

**25.** Would you rather get licked by **10** cats or get sat on by one large cat?

**26.** Would you rather have superpowers or have a superhero cat?

**27.** Would you rather be bitten hard by your cat or have to bite your cat gently?

**28.** Would you rather lick your cat's toys or eat its food?

**29.** Would you rather a cat that could clean your room or one that could do your homework?

**30.** Would you rather not do your homework for one night or not be able to play with your cat for five days?

**31.** Would you rather be scratched by your cat on your cheek or on your butt?

**32.** Would you rather your cat clawed you really hard or bit you really hard?

**33.** If you couldn't have a cat would you rather have a dog or a mouse?

**34.** Would you rather let your cat that played the violin or one that played video games?

**35.** Would you rather have a flying cat or a swimming cat?

**36.** Would you rather have a spooky cat who scared all your friends or a psychic cat who could tell your future?

**37.** Would you rather have a cat meowing very loud when you are trying to study for a big test or clawing you when you were trying to sleep?

**38.** Would you rather have a cat who ran very fast or a cat who jumped very high?

**39.** Would you rather dye your cat's fur pink or green?

**40.** Would you rather clean your cat's ears or your cat's nose?

**41.** Would you rather have a cat with no tail and long whiskers or a cat with a normal tail and no whiskers?

**42.** Would you rather name your cat after your father or after your mother?

**43.** Would you rather have your cat sneeze all the time or hiccup all day?

**44.** Would you rather sleep in the same bed with twenty cats or with your parents?

**45.** Would you rather have your cat wake you up in the morning or your alarm?

**46.** Would you rather your cat was able to read and type up your homework or was able to talk to humans and make you new friends?

**47.** Would you rather have a cat that can roller-blade or one that can ice-skate?

**48.** Would you rather have a bath with your best friend or with a stinky, dirty cat?

**49.** Would you rather find a thousand dollars or rescue a tiny kitten?

**50.** Would you rather have a black cat cross your path or be born on Friday the 13th?

Made in the USA
Las Vegas, NV
10 April 2024

88498486R00069